# STAR FALL IN A MIDNIGHT SKY

*Other Books by Denham Grierson
published by Coventry Press*

Turning in Time
Sharing Water by the River
Music From a Breaking Wave
Chronicles of Light & Air

POEMS OF LIGHT

# STAR FALL IN A MIDNIGHT SKY

DENHAM GRIERSON

Published in Australia by
Coventry Press
33 Scoresby Road
Bayswater VIC 3153

ISBN 9781922589316

Copyright © Denham Grierson 2023

All rights reserved. Other than for the purposes and subject to the conditions prescribed under the *Copyright Act*, no part of this publication may be reproduced, stored in a retrieval system, or transmitted in any form or by any means, electronic, mechanical, photocopying, recording or otherwise, without the prior permission of the publisher.

Catalogue-in-Publication entry is available from the National Library of Australia
http://catalogue.nla.gov.au

Cover design by Ian James – www.jgd.com.au
Text design EB Garamond

Printed in Australia

# Contents

| | |
|---|---|
| Foreword | 8 |
| Introduction | 10 |
| Acknowledgments | 12 |
|     Star Fall | 13 |
|     Who are my people | 14 |
|     Written down | 15 |
|     Autumn comes knocking | 16 |
|     Knowing less | 16 |
|     Harvest | 17 |
|     Chasm | 18 |
|     Trevally | 19 |
|     Consumerism | 20 |
|     Virus | 20 |
|     Nightmare prophesy | 21 |
|     Ecology | 22 |
|     Pond light | 22 |
|     Footy night | 22 |
|     Songs of praise | 23 |
|     Us | 24 |
|     At the end of the day | 25 |
|     Wondering | 26 |
|     Sprite | 27 |
|     Journey | 28 |
|     Dance | 29 |
|     Free | 29 |
|     Otherness | 30 |
|     Funeral | 31 |
|     Carol | 32 |
|     Not saying | 33 |

| | |
|---|---|
| Cancer | 34 |
| Suchness | 35 |
| Good Friday | 36 |
| Sonnet | 37 |
| Epitaph | 38 |
| Great Barrier Reef | 39 |
| Lament | 40 |
| Creation | 41 |
| Blessed are the light bearers | 42 |
| Lunch | 43 |
| Prayer | 44 |
| Thread | 45 |
| Gallery enchantment | 46 |
| Light | 47 |
| Away | 48 |
| Stenographer | 49 |
| Beginning | 50 |
| Embodiment | 51 |
| Election BBQ | 51 |
| Seasons | 52 |
| Impression | 53 |
| Somewhere | 53 |
| Sacrificial lamb | 54 |
| Centred | 55 |
| Puzzle | 56 |
| Candle | 57 |
| Twin | 58 |
| Flood | 59 |
| Song | 60 |
| After the flood | 61 |
| Joy in heaven | 62 |
| Now | 63 |
| Invitation | 64 |
| Music | 65 |
| Visitor | 66 |

| | |
|---|---|
| Mirror image | 67 |
| Soundings | 68 |
| If I had a wish | 69 |
| Today is moving day | 70 |
| Visitation | 71 |
| You also | 72 |
| Homeless | 73 |
| I missed it | 74 |
| Lolling | 74 |
| Purple bag with yellow string | 75 |
| Eminence | 76 |
| Beauty | 78 |
| Centre | 79 |
| Greatness | 80 |
| Dog pound day | 81 |
| Givingness | 82 |
| Freedom | 83 |
| Struggle | 83 |
| Travellers tale | 84 |
| Lego | 85 |
| Hubris | 86 |
| Impermanence | 87 |
| Shopping cart | 88 |
| Somewhere else | 88 |
| Jumping shoes | 89 |
| Entitlement | 90 |
| Breakneck speed | 91 |
| Sometimes | 92 |
| Milking shed | 93 |
| Kaleidoscope | 94 |
| Lotus | 94 |
| Blackberry harvest | 96 |
| In and out | 97 |
| Reflection on Ecclesiastes 3 | 98 |

# Foreword

In this new book of poems, Denham Grierson takes us from the magnificence of the expanding universe to the everyday magic of a string bag, from the enchantment of paint on canvas to the pain of a friend's cancer disclosure. In every one, we glimpse something of the holy.

Denham has invested his intellectual life in being an artisan theologian, mobilising the resources of faith to shape a more just and humane world. In these poems, we still encounter the cry for justice and a deep attending to the pathos of living; but we are invited into another kind of journey, into the apophatic poetic that comes 'out of the great unknowing we cannot name'.

Too easy formulas or clichéd Christianisms will no longer suffice. They are always in danger of destroying that which they presume to protect. The ever-present spark of the spirit refuses to be locked down by protective fear or insecure solidity. It flashes at the edges, emerges with each flicker of newness, and in simplicity sinks through the weave of our fabricated complexities.

Denham wants to call our attention to the sparks and flashes of the 'unspoken speed of eternity' which can never be captured in speech, text, or even thought, but are momentarily glimpsed in the spaces that open up with silence and deep listening. These poems – as only the poetic can do – courageously direct our attention to the unspeakable.

Emily Dickenson spoke of the haunting presence of the unspeakable.

> There is no Silence in the earth – so silent
> As that endured
> Which uttered, would discourage Nature
> And haunt the world

These poems point to this same sense of the illusive unutterable but not to a haunting but to a kind of dwelling, not to a threatening presence but to the uncontainable sacred to be found in every turn.

To be wondered at, and touched by, but never to be captured and contained.

These poems are fragile, wonderful and beautiful because they take us into the heart of human frailty, awe and desire, where war, illness, plague and age all threaten to steal life away. But the elusive presence of that which is beyond and beneath all remains. We share in the chemistry of eternity.

Andy Tiver

# Introduction

To the German philosopher Arthur Schopenhauer, the human person is the primary object of poetry, in actions, thought and emotions. The poet's aim is to make transparent – in concrete image, distinct and vivid – what lies in the abstract and universal nature we share. An attempt to interpret the mystery of our being and what it is.

From this perspective, poetry keeps the connection to time and space, to matter and substance, by the magic of novel perception, redefining the taken-for-granted. Seeking to say what language has never said before, to quote John Heath-Stubb.

It is the loss of a trustworthy reality that is the curse of our age, caught as it is in rapid change and flux. We struggle to measure the unique worth of the human. We do not know what to trust. We suffer from an obscuring, elusive reality. It was the poet Pablo Neruda who wrote, 'The poet who is not a realist is dead, and the poet who is only a realist is also dead'. Czeslaw Milosz agrees. Poetry, he declared, is the 'passionate pursuit of the real'.

Even so, Robert Frost was committed to a 'tantalising vagueness' that equally is characteristic of some of our finest poets. It is said of T.S. Eliot's poem, The Waste Land, that it is a poem about nothing. As was also said of Samuel Beckett's play, Waiting for Godot, emphasising Eliot's profound observation, 'The hint half guessed, the gift half understood is incarnation'. Poetry is inescapably real when it is anchored in what we call the human, recognising that the broadest definition of the human points, inescapably, beyond itself.

What emerges in the most real poems is an otherness, a transcendence, which places the poetic endeavour in the realm of mystery. We are unfathomable to ourselves, creatures striving for an understanding of our inner life that attempts, in multiple ways, to name itself.

It is this territory the poems in this collection explore. A pinball experience of ricochet from inner to beyond, real to imagined, matter to light and air, seeking substance, seeking interpretation, seeking understanding. In this environment, the task includes following the flow of inspiration, that volition, both conscious and unconscious, that reaches for a centre of gravity in contemporary experience. A telling of those things that matter. Light, illuminating the darkness, as from a star falling in a midnight sky.

# Acknowledgments

These acknowledgments seem repetitive. As always, thanks to Hugh McGinlay, Nicci Douglas, Coventry Press, my wife Mavis, my daughter Susan. Also the usual suspects, fellow poets John Cranmer and Andy Tiver, as well as a surrounding corpus of friends who offer support and criticism. To you all my great appreciation. And my delight also in this joint enterprise we call the poetic journey. Grace and Peace.

## STAR FALL

We live in a festival of stars
Children of time's womb
Fertile, dark and empty tomb
Nurturing billions of years

Cosmic web interlocking
Filaments of dark matter
Stitching out tendril data
Midwife to the birth of stars

Life bursting forth
Exploding energy awry
Crafting in the sky
Images of the Dreaming

Super-nova technicolour
Expanding through galaxies
Maelstrom of gravities
Rainbow snake profusion

Trillions of stars
Satin darkness in the heavens
Guiding with a yeasting leaven
Star fall in a midnight sky

## WHO ARE MY PEOPLE

Did the star falling out of the night sky
Trip over an asteroid
And, losing balance, fall into darkness

We, moving from one movie set, say of suburban existence
Suddenly entering another. A world of monsters
All guiding assurance gone. Leaving bewildered uncertainty

The anchor of knowing who are my people
Gone in an instance. Taking what we call reality
Disappearing with it. As if by magic

Looking back the falling star may see myriad family
Or, moving away from suburbia, we see looking back
A world that has died. No longer life or meaning

The present, unrecognisable territory
Inhabited by creatures who have an alien existence
An inner change of perception of social space

It is a matter of balance, this midnight glance
Leaving the world for another, unequipped
Yet carrying resources to discern pathways

The story of that time, that place, has made me
A picture album of a vanished past
Now is a new beginning. In an enchanted forest

## WRITTEN DOWN

I let them loose gently
Small silver bodies
Into the stream
Creatures translated free

Their life once released
Hidden, their own
Unbounded by expectation
Quicksilver in light

Doing their work
Whatever it is
For purposes unknown
Tasks imponderable

Only words in cohort
Merely affectations
Of immutable things
Slight tidings of joy

Smoke into air
Warmth into winter
Song into silence
Seed into soil

## *AUTUMN COMES KNOCKING*

Change arrives carried by the wind
Everywhere gold and russet leaves
Fluttering to earth. Autumn smells
Arrive for tea with news not unexpected

Somehow the birds adjust to a late
Coming of the sleepy dawn, delaying their
Morning songs a little, a sharper breeze
Wrapping around my legs as
Coming to full awareness, I fetch the morning paper

So the world turns, nothing fixed or final
Within the seasons, Nature or ours
The same overcome with newness again
Setting the task. Which news to ponder first

## *KNOWING LESS*

I know less every day
But there is more to learn they say
The James Webb telescope explores
Trajectories to distant shores

There the atoms gathered to be me
Exploded in a primal sea
Demonstrating on laboratory trays
That I know less every day

Get on the new celestial tram
Travel back to where it all began
Beyond galaxies like our Milky Way
I know less every day

Take me to the birthing minute
To gaze upon the opening gambit
To wonder at creation on its way
Confirming I know less every day

Knowing less makes me see
Simplicity beyond complexity
So liberated I go out to play
Relieved I know less every day

## HARVEST

La Niña storms ravage the ripened crops
Wheat sales heavy with defeated grain
The Southern paddocks
Disastrously flooded

Surrounding vineyards
Full grapes waiting harvest
As devastated by slashing rains
The crops destroyed

How serious? I ask Jessup
A death blow, he replies
The earth's yield irredeemably gone
No salvage possible

The second blow less visible
If we cannot break bread
And drink wine together
The harvest is truly lost

## CHASM

The stone wall lies broken, hammered along its length
Into disrepair, weakened by twisting vines and time's deprivations
No longer demarcating good and evil in its shattered rectitude
Overcome by unrelenting avarice and public deceit

Where are the builders who toiled ceaselessly
Driven by a vision of secure houses, safe habitats
Protected by truth saying and public care
Building a city over which the Prophet could pray

Where have they gone, the workers, the carers, the seers
Who has stolen the sense of reverence and responsibility
Substituting machines and expediency for human integrity
So the straight is made crooked, leading to land fill

It is hard to breathe in air choked with accumulation
Where the absence of justice makes hope an artefact
One looks in vain for those who fear God
And follow in the footsteps of the builders and carers

It is hard to trust the lying words of a betraying press
Bought off by those who only have one sense of profits
Where then those who love the earth and build
To nurture hospitality, when only the chasm awaits

## TREVALLY

It was a perfect cast. The line humming
Along the rod, the sinker high, defying gravity
Calling to hooks and bait to follow its wittering
Direction, plucked to song by a sea breeze passing

Falling strategically into the light green gutter
Between a wave on tip toe about to break and
The slow rising to maturity of a following one

Dropping into hazard of seaweed, fixed, rolling
Predatory currents, a surfeit of crab life

Resting steady, the line tightened by the reel's pull
Communication with the rod tip established
Settling to wait, subliminal messages travelling

The strike comes. The rod arches in reflex
Struck by a force, immediate, insistent, mobile

The struggle begins. Frantic reeling in, breath taut
Slow stepping backwards up the sandy slope
Twist, retreat, cat stillness, burst, check, twist

Tiredness creeping into assaulted wrists. The rod
Bending, springing back. The tortured line holding

The fish breaking out of the shallows, still fighting
Dragged onto the graveyard sands. Six pound

Pink in the late afternoon sun, scales glinting blue
The knife slits open the belly. Contents flung into the sea
A head soon follows, A squawking conceit of gulls descend

The slow slog home makes plain our fate
When urgent hunger dominates we take the bait

## CONSUMERISM

Consumer panic follows the news
Of mounting inflationary costs
Fifty-seven pieces of clothing
For each person a year
With a disposal rate of
Fifty-three items to follow
Making it clear how little we
Value what we have and our
Disinterest in why the cost is
So advantageous, inviting us
To unnecessary extravagance
Workers in Third World factories
Paid .02 of a cent for
Each item they produce
Being thrown away with their
Creations that we discard
So easily

## VIRUS

When the virus hit
The body, fully engaged
Had no thought but defence

Trapped inside its assaulted fabric
Helplessness overwhelmed the
Inner world of consciousness

Aches, pains, mental fatigue
Contributing to the inevitable
We live, tenuously, on borrowed time

## NIGHTMARE PROPHECY

Elements rage in concert, out of control
Tempestuous seas. Mountainous eruptions
A howling storm. A boiling surf
Flashing lightning. Hailing skies
Drum-roll thunder shattering our lives

Tumultuous force, utterly witless, that destroys
Nature beside itself with unbridled fury
Pandemics unleashed. Forest destruction spreads
Phenomena of gales. Rivers at spate. Consuming fire
Cyclonic plunder. Volcanic lava dire

Explosive energy ignescent. Cacophony of sound
Bringing down live wires, trees. Mud slides confound
As if the world's demonic, chaos in its grasp
Has been aroused to rapacious anger
Destroying all it sees in its insatiate hunger

Before such ferocity we are defenceless
The very earth itself begins to quake
Yet mindless we continue to enrage
The Leviathan breathing fire upon our crops
A stupendous, malign presence, crushing without stop

A small monk on a beach before a mounting wave
A pilot in the hurricane unsure he will be saved
A shepherd on a flooding wet-land plain
All these, and all of us along, victims in this disaster song
Refusing to acknowledge we were wrong

Foaming torrents. Rushing pitiless slaughter
Brings us to the pit of doom. Gaia convulsed by the torture
How can we face it, how meet its furious temperament
Terrible and indifferent in every killing form
Peace and enduring solitude, phantoms long since gone

## ECOLOGY

What is missing is
    An ecology of spirit
Un-seduced by things
    Trusting the essence
Of dimensions unseen
    Within a people who
Believe in each other


## POND LIGHT

The Egret and I stand
Looking across the pond, glistening with sky
He within, I without. Celebrating


## FOOTY NIGHT

Registering on the train monitor
Joining an excited crowd of festooned tribes
Some will laugh. Some cry

## SONGS OF PRAISE

The huge Cathedral imposing in its height
Gathered organ chords and vocals
Into its stained glass light

The congregation with fervour
Professed traditional faith
Hymns of centuries over

Enshrining a universe long gone
Words passing along the T.V. glass
Presenting a vision of a world time passed

Angels, thrones, kingdoms, a distant heaven
Held immobile by ancient words
Reinforced by mitre, gesture, obscure creeds

They sang of the unchanging one
As if they really knew
Not of the Spirit travelling to the new

The weight of pomp and circumstance
In plain sight for contemporaries to see
For all its magnificence it did not speak to me

## US

The microscopic insect
    flashes
Across the virginal whiteness

A communication
    lost

    The Word gone
before comprehension

    All as before
    A nothingness
    Without trace

But there is the page
    the pen
the vanished moment

    I did not put ink
    upon the paper

    Listening
to the unspoken speech
    of eternity

    In stillness
        In silence
    Waiting

## AT THE END OF THE DAY

At the end of the day
When darkness has dominion
I sit around an inner camp fire
To warm myself over the day's events

Roasting small pieces of experience
On a stick of reflection
Tasting the buried meaning of each piece
Entering in to deeper awareness

Again the day opens up its gifts
Offering what was missed the first time
Tantalising aroma of hidden mystery
To complement the taste of living

Friendly fire lights the candle
Of the day's recollection
My life's substance being slowly consumed
Knowing itself by the shedding of light

The day rested, enjoyed, cleansed
Sleep comes to prepare tomorrow

## *WONDERING*

Strange to be up again
In the small hours
Without sleep or purpose
Did someone call

Falling into a darkness
Needing the attention
Of a friend
Who would come if called

Prayer however cannot
Change what is inevitable
Or reverse the damage
Of neglect once afflicted

Even the silence knows this
Making no response
To my query of why
Urging me, nonetheless, to hope

For nothing is at risk
Nothing threatened in the
Small hours of wondering
Except faith

## SPRITE

It is cause and effect that is
The corset constraining our breathing out
Producing as it does a world of
Dry predictability, dark chimney stack stain
Obliterating the colours of the morning sun
Offering certainties of lifeless ash
As nourishment for the living of our days

Not knowing of that spirit that ignores
The inevitability of time, space,
and causality
Breaking into clouded dreams, the cry from
Far distant hills, ice free flow over
Crowded rocks, bird song at the twilight hour
The inward stirring in the unborn child
Whispering the story of becoming whole

Music of unwritten symphonies that do not
Need straight lines and scored notes to
Sing new songs in our hearts, or to break
Open the cages, breach the locks, set free
Those imprisoned by inevitability, those fearful
Of what breaks into ruled securities without knocking
Scattering the pieces moved by ordered necessity

I am not convinced our real life is
Bound by that which seems determined
Too much mischief and delight dances
On the edge of things, surprising as a raffle win
An act of unexpected kindness, dribble of cereal milk
Upon the morning chin
And the gentle, suffering trace in all creative buoyancy

Wait for the presence then, that sneaks alongside
And winks, dissembling in the structured reverence
Of solemn assemblies and pious performance
As free as the capering winds, knocking
On window panes later and later
Reminding us that what is truly real
Lives in the abandonment of uninhibited laughter

## JOURNEY

It is the case that
In the life of faith
You are always beginning

Leaving a hut of understanding
On a brisk Autumn day
To set out again on a new track

Not doubting direction but substance
Love after all is not worth anything
Without trust, or endurance, or forgiveness

So hiking boots, staff, travelling supplies
Off again, casting aside dried certainties
Filled with a nameless excitement

As if past the Pepper-corn tree, around the next bend
Or breasting the rise above waving paddocks
All will become clear and reassuring

It is the journey. Loving the questions
Being confronted by surprise. Overcome with joy
Why did I not see it long ago

## DANCE

Outside, nose pressed to the glass
Not hearing the orchestra, or choir
Mystified by the dancer's whirling steps
With little comprehension of what transpires

Even so, at the cafe table, he told me proudly
How religiously unmusical he was
Dismissing totally that which seemed to him
The senseless acts of those addicted to floss

He who had not entered in, or ever danced a waltz
Oblivious to the rhythm of transporting sound
The inner essence of the dance of time
The celebrative pattern of life's sacred ground

## FREE

How much can one carry
Or should. Or needs to
To be equipped. To survive

The dream reoccurs
What I seek to take
Does not fit into my case
Do I need a bigger case
I cannot manage
Or reduce what I want to keep

What after all is necessary
What is enough
What really matters

She has sold most of her possessions
To fit into one room in the Home
'I feel free' she told me

## *OTHERNESS*

The religious dimension is not susceptible to dismissal
Its mystical ground is an immediate presence
Of the Divine. In Nature, community, and direct address

The moment before God is not to be rejected
As polemic, delusion, or wish fulfilment
Its transformative power is adduced in personal change

Its impact is relational, the salience of engagement
Compounded of inner speech, profundity of mystery's meeting
Self authenticity within unspoken dialogue

Personal, social, historical, as compelling as community
That organic belonging, embracing what gives meaning
To the sense of self, named by a people who are family

If speech falters, demonstration remains elusive, testimony frail
This is the face of that dark knowledge which is knowing
By not knowing, or controlling, or possessing. Which is a gift of
Grace

## FUNERAL

Usually we only bury saints
No other kind of human
Spoken of at funerals

Today was the exception
Today we honoured a saint
And damned her with faint praise

Reducing her life to stories
Eccentric actions, offering advice
And comic episodes remembered

No mention of her faith
A lifetime of worship
A loving embrace of the helpless

Her care of the family
Unfailing empathy
And simple kindness

As if in this world
Goodness must not be spoken of
Lest it bring shame upon us

## *CAROL*

'In the beginning was the Word.' The Gospel of John

Was ever, was ever, was ever
Do not contemplate never
Before the heart's throb, and sung carol
Every jot and every tittle
Before the fire, the chair, the cot
Always coming, never not
Before time's place for us to gather
Always ever, always ever, always ever

Was ever, was ever, was ever
For the hopeless and the clever
Deep within the core of earth
Creation's groaning coming forth
Always was, always is, never never
Was ever, was ever, was ever
Within the blackest black whole
Precursor of the sacred scroll

Bell call pure. Clearly the Word was heard
Was heard, was heard, was heard

## NOT SAYING

Can everything be said
By saying nothing
That silence that speaks volumes
Avoiding exhortation, rhetoric, or piety
Without comment
Gathering power from an everything
Unspoken

They gathered rocks to stone her
He knelt and wrote on the ground
Saying everything by saying nothing
Taking from them self-righteousness
Drawing a line in the sand
Standing before judgment voiceless
An unspoken everything

It is silence that is determinative
Leaving everything unsaid
By means of nothing uttered
A force that has no centre
To destroy by argument
Of any kind
Saying all needed

## CANCER

The cancer has returned
The second time, implacable and stern

My life now rests on a scalpel edge
Beyond prayer, and pleading and pledge

Is this the point where angels dance
Its fatal thrust, destined or chance

I rise into another beckoning day
Uncertain at work or rest or play

Will there be another cruel awakening
Obverse of my hopeful wishing

Or can the surgeon be trusted
We got it all, the fatal verdict busted

Will I live three score years and ten
Can I travel joyously to my end

## SUCHNESS

Worship comes to Sundays
As light to morning
Swans to evening water
Ants to spilled honey
Like the process in flow
We cannot change what simply is

There are dimensions of the mind
No longer permitted to us
Slayed by the tyranny of reason
Unwilling to permit creation's novelty
That brings forth out of nothing
A newness sparkling in evolution's sun

I have watched the seasons of my life
Change without the power either to control
Or understand, since there are depths
Unfathomable in the moment's touch
Escaping into fresh experience
Emerging slyly when the deed is done

Reaching unofficial ends, spontaneously
Repeating the same words in every home
Telling the same stories in vellum tomes
Suffering is not a habit into which we fall
To shape our soul for virtue, but the text
Of what we cannot govern on the way

So I turn again to the word spoken
The word written, the word lived
Knowing what cannot be expected
That thread that binds the whole
The light the candle nurtures
The breath we cannot take until we breathe

## *GOOD FRIDAY*

I have tried to explain
With no valid arguments
Or compelling reasons

A slashing rain
Destroying ripened crops
Is as explainable

Vineyards matured to harvest
See their fruit destroyed
By whim of a sharp climate change

And he dies
Waiting in an ambulance for hours
Outside a plague assaulted hospital

I build the blocks upward
Watching them fall down
For want of plausibility

Trying to read the lines
Of destiny on my palm
Is just as profitable

Questions without answers
Stalk us on the razor's edge
Where we huddle to keep warm

## SONNET

The message was more like a plea
A seeking for a road to follow
Across the spreading plains a plague
That puts at jeopardy tomorrow

Tell them I wrote, the message said
Tell them my fields are lying fallow
I cannot meet you at the feast
Though all is right and all is mellow

I have not yet come full to harvest
No gifts to bring, no insights to be shared
But I am not without a hope that's living
I work with joy in every way implied

Within my fallow field I found a treasure
That gives me peace in all ways I can measure

## *EPITAPH*

Mischievously, put this on my tombstone

> JESSUP
> WAS A BASTARD
> AS WE ALL ARE

A tribute to the deep sensibility
That understands our true estate
However ironical in form

These days only saints are buried
Often to the sounds of their favourite song
The shallow soil of secularism
Offering no promise of flowering

No, said Jessup, we cannot claim
Significance for our own existence
Or its redemption, in word or act
We are too compromised by ambiguity

Instead we celebrate a welcome
We do not earn
And should not expect
This love has the last word

## GREAT BARRIER REEF

The reef is spawning
Birthing its tomorrow
With exuberance and abundance

Hundred of thousands of organisms
Acting unified, as one creature
Exploding creative activity
A cascading moment of kairos

Bursting, thousands upon thousands
Upon thousands of eggs into the warm
Mother environment of the
Waiting sea, coming to be

Life emerging conscious of itself
Vital, dynamic, novelty rampant
Rising into embodiment
All life, all being, all something particular

Potent and overwhelming
Declaring its life principle
Life beyond all limitation
Being born into becoming

This prodigious day of the year
When faith asks
What more is needed to believe
Before this testimony, life coming to itself

Touching the ground of all things
A springboard into the idea
Of all things awakening in the mind of God

Cloud burst affirming life
Primal display of the cosmic yes
Breaking all barriers to existence
The reef is spawning

## *LAMENT*

I awake to the rhetoric of war
To lies of its nobility
Helpless commentary
Castrated by death
An unending smell of corruption
The stamp of feet, the march of folly
Men and women dying in futility
Tears drowning the hopes of mothers
Children clutching broken lives forever

And politicians practising their pitch
Of what they are doing for us
As they bury my son and my daughter
For all of them are my children
And I can do nothing
Even prayer is dust before
Merciless brutality and cruel pride
And on this day of remembrance
The shine of medals will piece
Our hearts again
For they change nothing

## CREATION

Where is the song before it is written
The painter's creation before canvas conceived
Where are the clouds before their appearing
Where is the sunset not yet perceived

Where is the story not yet in the telling
The concept of ballet before the first dance
Where is the fragrance before the breeze carried
Where is the web before spider enhanced

Where was the smile before Leonardo
Michelangelo saw David in anonymous stone
Where is the oak before the seed planted
Where was my life when I was alone

Before is the chance that grows into creation
Out of the ether the form comes to be
Not subject to reason or logic or knowing
Birthed out of a fecund, sun dancing sea

Here is the star born in eternity
Here is the light that ensures that we see
The heart of expression, the act of creation
In this our uniqueness, our coming to be

Where intuition before the imagining
Where is the moment before the free act
God's touch in our breathing, creating, conceiving
Out of the nothingness, unshackled by fact

Here is the centre of that which we carry
Deep in the metric of blood and bone
Made in the image of a Creator
Making reality's substance our own

Where were we then before our enfleshment
Coming, coming, coming to be
Where the completion in the becoming
The on-going creation that lets us see

## *BLESSED ARE THE LIGHT BEARERS*

The control switch turns. The light withdraws
Losing intensity, growing paler and small
Darkness encroaches, subduing the light
Hungry for conquest. The light goes in the hall

A twitch of the kaleidoscope tube changes reality
Multi glass fragments, bright light infused
Perfectly balanced, judiciously refined
Change in an instant. A new pattern outlined

Light blazes through the symbolically round
Rose window, icon of a redeemed surround
Sending its splendour into the sanctuary
Illuminating its otherness, its warmth on display

Light that gives life in extended bouquet
Blessed the light bearers for each in its way
Brings joy and gladness in outreaching array
Whose giving keeps black darkness at bay

We watch dawn light creep across paddocks grey
Chasing the spectre of night time away
The orange orb rising into endless blue sky
Another day dancing with time's butterflies

## LUNCH

When we talked about lunch
I did not expect salmon
Squid rings and brown ale

Nor the news of the return of cancer
A pending operation without definition
An account of another fall

It was the assault on our mortality
We supped on to the sound
Of pattering rain outside

The basket of petunias had faded
Sharp, perked ears of the dog
Listening for messages

Ours already delivered
After the fish and the ale
The rain falling, enthusiastically

## PRAYER

Prayer is not primarily, or even, about words
More a field of focus, a fulfilling reciprocity
Not shaped by the sacredness of space alone
A dwelling intensely in the humble ordinary
Less than an address sent out to another
Active suspension of the flow of self-possession

A resonance of the You into which I meld
(And You, blossoming in my inner being in return)
Not offering praise or solving problems
Resting thankfully, a place of meeting, of binding wounds
As in all intimacy, a sharing
Rain drift on a soft, warm, summer day

A sense of wonder and delight
A tremor of fear and doubt
A certainty of intent, a caress
A rainbow fantasy of Otherness
The reach of now, of last resort
An urgency of food and drink, denied, sought

The means of honouring life's gift
And life itself, renewed again
As if reborn, the breath of spirit
Coming to its heart as one shared beat
You are there before we call
Our cry a fundament of longing

The prodigal's return
The welcome embrace
The still point

## THREAD

A single glistening thread bright in the sun
Suspended almost a metre above the carpet
Spun out of the depths of an industrious spider
Perhaps building a complex bridge for inter-action
Driven by life imperatives to survive
To spin a trap for careless unsuspecting flight
Small creatures destined not to cross but to disappear

We carry within us the same hope and vision
Of significant constructions that will ensure
Not only the satisfaction of bodily necessity
But a deep hunger to create a thoroughfare
A passage open to communication, to intimacy
Where we can find a gossamer fineness
Meaning shared that glistens brightly in the light

## GALLERY ENCHANTMENT

*Before us waiting. Reassurance*
*Gleaming on the brass nobs*
*Of the studded doors*
*Into the Gallery's promise*
*Mirrors of reflected inwardness waiting*
*Contagion of perception's vision*
*Beyond the sign, Masks must be worn*

The stifled air in the Gallery
Seems dedicated to stillness
Faint smell of paint infiltrating
Into awareness, the long walk
To the Hall's far wall
Bewitched by lesser creations
Our gaze clear, fixed, certain

The large canvas reigns on
The West wall, commanding all else
That appears trivial
By contrast with its sovereignty
Time has no purchase here
No opinion can enhance or diminish
The greatness of its embodiment

The ideation itself before us. Beyond reason
Doubt and error, spirit unshackled
Waging unequal war
By gentle purity
Carrying a healing consolation
That brush and paint and colour
Cannot deliver. Except by enchantment

## LIGHT

Moods are as choking as smoke
As smothering as clouds
Hiding alternatives, obscuring options
Trustworthy as quicksand

They come unbidden, without warning
Blocking the sun, eroding confidence
Carrying the weight of ancient indiscretions
Recalling to mind unforgiven offences

Escape routes are few, duration unknown
As if a spread net shuts in despair
Or perhaps a sense of hopelessness
Mounting endless flights of stairs

That is why light is hope
The light that opens up another story
Of freedom and forgiveness and newness again
The light of life, of a fresh way, of glory

The light that comes with no bill to pay
That brings to sight the dawning beyond night
The light of venture, of tomorrow, of healing
That casts out the darkness, forever bright

## *AWAY*

I want to run away
To escape
From the weight
Of expectations

To sit without agendas
Or the need to justify
Idleness

To feel free
Of responsibility
And duties
Not to worry or fuss
Or fear

But it is futile
Wherever I run
I carry myself with me

## STENOGRAPHER

Is the poetic impulse a force of nature
That permits no argument or dispute
Arriving fully grown, complete like
Pallas Athene emerging from the head of Zeus

Carrying its own agenda, its chosen sculptured form
Seizing the pen and settling busily to work
Leaving the poet aside, bewildered and constrained
Writing what he does not own or know

Stating what he cannot speak
Following a hidden persona deep within
A daemon, who cannot be restrained
Expressing a power not subject to control

This creative explosion comes to expression
Within the poet, captive to an alien will
His work, yes, outside of which he stands
A participation mystique defying explanation

As if the creative flood that flows on a river bed
Of communal unconsciousness comes
In image, metaphor, and myth, to give reassurance
To the everlasting tide in which we swim

## *BEGINNING*

It is not the usual path that finds direction
For your need, your call, your inner task
You can look intensely into pictured worlds
And scripted text, stylised by embellishments
And find nothing

Yet in gathering sticks, delivering mail
Washing the dog, cleaning the pantry floor
You may be staring at what awaits you
Reaching into the hidden vault of your being
Opening the way you seek

Not recognised for what it is
Cloaked by the ordinary, the mundane
A key is not required, only readiness
A hunger to set out and find
What makes life spin

Even then only a beginning
Preparations need to be made, thoughtfully
For there is no map, no guiding instructions
Only a compelling impulse to set forth
On that journey to find your Self waiting

## EMBODIMENT

Young earnest commentators
Urge the efficacy of new apps
Requiring of me only eyes and ears
The fingers and a credit card perhaps

Sitting in enforced isolation
Captive ear buds and screen
Without access to activity
I wonder where my body's been

Denied touch and hugs and kisses
Disengaged from action's song fest
Required only to be passively present
I wonder what my body meant

## ELECTION BBQ

BBQ service on election day
The long queue snaking around
The block, asking for sauce and onions

Establishing a necessary ambience
Welling up in a gum-scented Australian-ness
That carries tribal heritage

Bewildering newcomers from other lands
Untouched by the mystique of
Voting in nostalgic aromas
Reassurance of election day coronas

## SEASONS

We see only so far
Seeing what we need
An explanation deemed sufficient
Secure capture of necessity

To our eyes four seasons
Named, defined, repeated
We penetrate so far
And are defeated

Gondara people see further, deeper
Seven seasons tell their story
Of plentiful supply in sequence
A nurture greater than necessity

Frazer Island people persevere longer
Nature more profoundly read
Thirteen seasons offer their plenitude
An embrace more complete again

Insight breeding an expanding sentience
More intimate, beyond mere occupation
The seasons of our life
Richer, poorer, poor by what we notice

How we look and understand
How we knock and enter

## *IMPRESSION*

The cobwebs of the day in myriad patterns
Blue, red, teal and, sometimes, yellow flashes
In constant interaction, election fashion
On coats, scarves, beanies, modulated splashes
Disguising in their brightness the hidden grimness
The tone, the pain, the tapestry of life and death
Queues of determination, commitment, bewildedness
Laying out the jigsaw of a nation's wealth
A fervent searching for a hoped-for future
Beside the trampled verges, the roadside kill
The pleading for understanding
Scribes write the stories of release and torture

## *SOMEWHERE*

They danced, light bodied, soft footed
Silently upon the shining forest floor
Towards, away, around, duet of grace
Sprite-like in all forms, as before

Slipping between thin myrtle trunks undetected
As old men, white beards, capped heads
Blowing smoke rings, seated on fallen trunks
Talked of lost children and the war

A drifting fog obscured the hollow
Moon light stretching to iron mountain tops
Where giants carried my bed, O long ago
Memories now lost across the dingo flats

The music goes merrily on, in cold and heat
Leaving no room for loss or grief
Calling in our blood's sweep
You can visit again in drowsy sleep

## SACRIFICIAL LAMB

The sheep had been herded into pens. Ready
Foot rot had spread. A day of the sharp knives
Each sheep pushed to the moment of surgery
Hard cardboard crust cut away. Blood flowing freely
An antiseptic wash. They prod foot away. Whimpering
A blazing sun sucking us dry to the marrow of our bones

The specialist. Small, friendly, eager
Ready with knife and teeth for castration day
Slicing into scrotum skin. Pulling testicles free
With his teeth. Spitting them away
Blood slowly caking his face. Making his hair stiff
A blazing sun sucking us dry to the marrow of our bones

It was a day of clippers. The dag residue
Matted to the wool, infected by bush flies
Was cut away, sliced back to the haunches
The sheep fearful and bewildered
Venting their distress as the clippers did their work
A blazing sun sucking us dry to the marrow of our bones

In the shade of the shearing shed at day's end
We put ice cold cans to our foreheads
Pouring liquid down parched throats. A long day of drenching
Pushing and pulling sheep into the sheep dip baths
Prodding them below the surface to cover every part
A blazing sun sucking us dry to the marrow of our bones

In the shadow I wondered if the one we called Shepherd
Had days of knives and clippers. Surgically acting
For the health of the flock. Inflicting suffering and
Pain because of hard love necessity
Attending to the helplessness and need thereby
A blazing sun sucking him dry to the marrow of his bones

Jessup's long shadow fell through the doorway
He stepped into the shed, brushing dust from his clothes
Sitting on a hay bale he joined the conversation
He noticed my depression. Is it necessary, I asked
All this suffering. You look beat, he said
Come for dinner tonight, He paused. We are having lamb

## CENTRED

The great lie is that knowledge
Tells us what we need to know
The truth is that without it
We have no means to grow

Our truth, or lack of truth
For at our deciding centre
We believe, against the odds
That honour is our anchor

Not understanding the paradox
Of give and take
We are the servants of integrity

## PUZZLE

He was a former colleague
Who, as far as could be judged
Lived faithfully undisturbed
Living in a middle ground
Untroubled by anxieties or unfathomable
Questions, enfolded by an assured
Predictability

He gathered dry stems of common-places
Tying them together with grey cliches
Offering them as a gift of bright yellow daffodils
Emissaries of a new Spring freshly born
Singing of new beginnings, newly cut endings
And I wondered why he could not tell
The living from the dead

## CANDLE

The digital world multiplies its complexities
Its intricate wonders giving birth to the banal
In glittering confusion, confounding choice

Unable to cultivate in us a comfort of silence
Offering its multitudinous attractions to disguise
Our malnutrition, to fill up the emptiness of affluence

The eternal symbol of the candle
Sheds its light by the strike of a match
Not by electronic extravagance

An invitation to meditation, stillness
And reflection by its gentle radiance
That overcomes the darkness of nothingness

So simple a creation, pushing us to see
Simplicity as the true path of the soul
Leading to entrancing, warming illumination

## TWIN

If you have shared a womb you will understand
The sudden moment of absence, icy wasteland of a loss
Of something precious
An emanation from a sub-conscious memory trace
A nameless space empty of evidential reality
Like a squall swiftly passing on a black cloud day

If my sister had lived she would have saved me
From locker room misogamy, gender superiority evidenced by
Jibe, joke, and judgments in cohorts
Of synthetic *camaraderie*, hiding our doubts
Giving no thought to the reduction of wholeness
In our sanctioned blindness

You would understand also the threat
Of being crushed, cramped, confined
In space reduced by another
Claustrophobic, creating by reaction
A defensive independence, protective and resistant

If my sister had lived she would have saved me
From the defensiveness against forced proximity
Freeing my *anima* from fear of a presence
Who brought to intimate closeness a
Caring, consoling, and considered affection
Reconciling me not to her but to myself

## *FLOOD*

The streets decorated by hillocks of debris
Along avenue stretches of wreckage strewn
Line growth of tides, brown marking all the houses
Now demeaned by filth and ruin

Only a week after the new carpet laid
Joe had his front lawn top dressed
And Mrs Ryan placed her family photos
In the shed, now sodden and despoiled

Wherever you look, loss and suffering
Corpses of dead dreams, gravestones of endeavours
A lone figure by the oak, looking at his boots
Coated with slime, crying in sharp Autumn weather

There arises a faint mist escaping the fetid smell
Of despair, a bewilderment beyond comprehension
Denial leaking out of Canberra corridors
The Government signing a new list of coal projects

## SONG

The morning chorus tunes up
As light creeps across the Wetland ponds
Red sun rising up, stretching out, over
Morning again the song sings, come, come alive

My father used to sing in the bathroom
Splashing water into his face, sweeping sleep away
As unselfconsciously his delight escaped
The cage of night, his spirit rejoicing unrestrained

On chilly mornings church bells rang across
The city announcing another beginning
I listened to the bird-song filled with
Novelty and joyousness. I felt their bursting exuberance

Perhaps a conceit but that mantle of joy
Seems muted and absent in a secular, perplexed world
For why give thanks and praise when
There is no Other to whom greeting can be given

I miss the plain-song of praise spreading its joy
Over the earth, shouting another day has begun
See the light, feel the warmth, the embrace of hospitality
Get up, sing, dance, be free. Modernity cannot kill this song

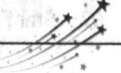

## AFTER THE FLOOD

The ancient wooden church
Flood cleansed of all
Human habitation bows
Damp and bewildered
Above the ecclesiastical pile
Of its possessions waiting removal

A throw away society
Empty of all defining identity
Marked now by mud stain
And a sober, futureless despair
An enigma that falls heavily
Into the sodden coils of restless uncertainty

How is it possible to be liberated
From something to which commitment
Was never made, or a mode of
Being in the world never experienced
The congregation now gone to saving work
Helping the afflicted, homeless, and lost to survive

## JOY IN HEAVEN

Jessup and I lingered at the grave side
As the other mourners moved away
A soft wind causing my gown to flap
Riffing through the sheets of the eulogy

His neighbour's two year old daughter
Jessup's God-child, killed by a disease
The doctors could not stop, or barely name
Joy and possibility gone, said Jessup

I wonder if they will have trumpets
At the gates, red balloons, her favourites
Certainly they will have festive gaiety
And she will run, clapping her hands

We walked up the dirt path
To the waiting car among the gums
Bowed by a shared grief that has no words
The beat of our hearts telling us the time

## NOW

The accumulation of things precious
Can only end with dispossession
Years piled up to be discarded
Without weight or meaning, upon the nature strip
Dumped into land fill, that cemetery of dreams
Where lie abandoned and undiscovered
The essence of what we hoped for, hopelessly

Space has no intimacy, how can it be close
There is no meeting in aloneness, cold and forbidding
We desire warmth, embrace of glowing coals
The smell of baking bread, the glass half full
So that we can manage to stay bonded
To each other, breaking new bread, sharing old wine
Together, in a humanness coming to be

What we hunger for can only be found
In silence, stillness and humility
Those values of presentness that escape
Us in getting and holding and demanding
The congress of swallows gathered without words
Watching my coming, wait to flee as one
For only together, as a flock, are we complete

In the flood even the trees are not safe
In the drought the billabong vanishes away
In the fire there is only fire
In the cyclone directions have no veracity
Where can we stand? Where can we go
If we will not admit death is consuming
At all cost, to no end

What matters at the peak or in the chasm
In winning and losing, in acquiring knowledge
If we do not know our true state of being
Not reading the writing in the sand
Nor caring for frightened children in the night
Let those without sin cast the first stone

I do not presume to be predictive
The sunset clause already set in place
In our turn we come to judgment
No further than a mirror, the beat of time
What we have is now, this Summer
Autumn, Winter, Spring, of time's reflection
The new beginning. The moment before God

## *INVITATION*

The invitation was simple
Just bring yourself
No presents
Plan to stay
There will be much celebration

I remember it well
Although it is still to come
A banquet unsurpassed
Substance of all our hopes
Providence of things to come

## MUSIC

Music is the universal language
Spirit of the spheres. Cosmos owned
Spirit of time's dance across the ages
Marrow running through our very bones

Trickle of the flute across the scattered stones
Voice of the thunder high in the sky
Solace of the heart from heath to throne
Laughter's delight, sorrow's tearful cry

Singing of the day before and of tomorrow
Celebrating life in all its forms
Source of the song of nightingale and sparrow
Shaping our humanness which its magic transforms

Giving to our awareness lilting delight
To our steps bright patterns shaped by purpose
Leading us by hand into the light
By sleight of hand, the whimsy of the circus

And when they cannot sleep we sing a song
That reassures and soothes their anxious frown
Companion of each breath, the inner throng
Hope, joy, and love we have always known

The stupendous gift, heart of each life-time
The humming of the soul at rest
Beyond the rhythm's beat, the pulsing rhyme
The language spoken in creation's nest

## VISITOR

What did he want? When he came
Are you sure it was him after all
Recognised without doubt
No one seemed to know him well
Unsure of what he wanted

Was he a teacher? A wise man? A healer
Determined to slay all ignorance
Perhaps a bearer of judgment on our
Refusal to acknowledge how things are
Some of you, I know, thought of him
As an angel in disguise, an agent of Destiny

Others, a messenger of news waited for
A poet, a storyteller of tales about
A mysterious reality deep within
Was he a recruiter gathering travellers
For a fateful journey. Seeking soldiers
For a holy war. Or for a pilgrimage to
Investigate re-fertilising wastelands

Some thought him a dance master and magician
Others a mystery, a disconcerting otherness
I cannot make much sense of the confusion
Although those who followed seemed transformed
Exhibiting a growing certainty about his offer
What did he want? What did he ask? Who was he
Did he ask for me? Leave an invitation to join him
Do you think we will see his like again
Did he tell us what we needed to know

## MIRROR IMAGE

We do not have to struggle
To find our image in a mirror
The struggle is to understand
What it is we see

The ghostly appearance without depth
Is transparent, easily discerned
Giving itself, elusively, to be seen
A visibility troubling unlearned

Does this image offer one's self
To say, I exist, somebody, more than a clone
A becoming evident, a revealing
Seeking beauty, wanting to be known

Persevering in our search
For an identity of oneself, icon of the human
A hunger of the species to name itself
Significant, worthy to be loved, within communion

## SOUNDINGS

The mirror does not lie
A burnt out case
Skin stretched across
Sharpened bones, brittle
Under time's growing weight
The stride now a step
The hand trembles
Lifting a cup to dry lips

But each morning the bells
As always ring out
Listen to the promise
Resonating with assurance
Telling of resurrection warmth
Chiming out of the energies
That bind all things together
Tolling again, all will be well

## IF I HAD A WISH

If we had seven wishes granted
Or one or two or three
To take them would be foolish
How do we know what we want to be

Only trial and error or mistakes help us see
What we want now is what we ought to flee
Each moment a newness, each act another road
Whose end is never clear whether earth or sky or sea

The task of each deciding, the fateful grasp of will
Is an elusive mystery, enigmatic in its glance
Following a trajectory which time and living spills
Wrapped in choice, chance, and changing circumstance

If I had to make a wish
Pressured by some compelling force
I would ask for freedom to choose
Commitment on my charted course

## TODAY IS MOVING DAY

The wondrous mosaics of Pompeii uncovered
Under metres of volcanic ash remained unchanged
The colour had not bled under extreme heat
Stones remained set and unmoved
Timeless beauty incapable of movement
Incapable of being other than it is

Doctrines and creeds are equally set in time
Immoveable, locked securely in place by
The press and reverence of tradition
As set in relationship as mosaic floors
Beauty and utility unquestioned
Equally incapable of being different
Incapable of being other than they are

There is little life here for the shaping of a future
Only a record of once upon a time
A place we can visit but not enter
Words have died, mummified by immutability
Telling of a world view once compelling
Now without life. No flowers grow here

We are children of a wind, blowing where it will
Feeling its breeze on our skin, its song in our ears
Today is moving day. To seek a new world
Opening up fertile ways of risk and fresh adventure
Defined by flow, convulsion, and discovery
Of that at the heart of all that grows. That reaches out
That travels windswept, into the yet to be

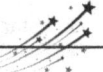

## VISITATION

The reminiscence wandered
Permitted when a ninety-ninth birthday
Completes a narrative cycle

A life scratched out of the dust
Of a World War. A marriage
Out of pieces of circumstance

Looking back on poverty
Lived in a fog of misunderstanding
On a farm without spoken words of love

The slow growth, the sudden flowering
Setting out on a journey of discovery
Among books providing food and drink

Thorns and thistles of the human kind
Three children who walked a hard road
While their mother, persisting, conquered

A career, seeking justice for her kind
Spirit indomitable, unbroken by loss or fear
Remembering beyond failure, trumpets in the morning

And now, grasping the fading light with recognition
Telling a story shaped by a hunger to be known
As someone who did not, in the heat of the day, falter

## *YOU ALSO*

I am unfathomable to myself
But so are you unfathomable
To yourself and also me

A mysterious country
Never mapped or known securely
Although traversed frequently

As if the sensibilities we share
Are deceptions of sense
Untranslatable in living time

Why we imagine we can translate
The untranslatable
I do not know

But living without communion
Is worse than dying intestate
Confessing nothing to posterity

Let us travel together joyously
Merging our hopes and dreams
Your hand is warm and grips mine

## HOMELESS

A grey winter fog hangs menacingly
Over the Wet-land scene
Swallowing flocks, silencing song
A dead blanket, a suffocating screen

The sun has its own light, the moon borrows
Without strength to conquer the night
To part the curtains bringing blindness
Crowding space, prohibiting sight

Under its concealing cover they sleep
In streets and lanes, cold, hungry, friendless
Hard pavements, damp blankets, paralysed
By need, numbed by trauma and stress

Cars frosted with ice enclose families
Who live and sleep in poverty's cage
Homeless without hope or defence
Already condemned by the city to this grave

A power crisis strikes the suburbs
Heaters cool, the temperature falls
In the desolation of the streets
Where can they go? Who can they call

## I MISSED IT

I missed it, not by intent
The screamer in the goal square
A venomous insult, the feathered slight
I was distracted, although there
Missing the offer of a life
The slow deterioration of another
Eschewing hunger and need
The true case of anger, greed
Black clouds, rising wind, blinding sand
Embrace of a loving touch not seen
Even the chance of greatness unrecognised
With open eyes and slumbering heart
    No, I mean the gift, the focus
    The love, the beauty of the crocus

## LOLLING

She was very insistent
There is not enough lolling going on
The magic Kingdom of idleness
Nothing much happening, going on

The kayak drifting under shadowing trees
To no purpose. Being mesmerised by a candle's
Flickering flame, without intent. A cushioned
Gaze into nothing much. Family photo
Album idly explored. Flicking through
Fashion books. Wondering about stardust
A dedicated hanging loose, doing little
The pause of breaking day indifference

I am serious, she said, yawning
We must learn the art of leaning back
I gave her opinion due thought
Just now, however, I am taking up the slack

## PURPLE BAG WITH YELLOW STRING

I wonder if you knew, you on one side, you on the other
Untying the yellow string on the purple bag
They would sing, the fluttering dancing things within
Leading us down the road with burbling springs

To where the Wizard and the Hag gave us with yellow string
A purple bag telling us to untie the yellow string
If so they would sing, the fluttering dancing things
Leading us down the road with burbling springs

To where the Magician and the Fool sing together
Purple bag with yellow string, open so we can enter in
To find the dancing things with fluttering wings
To hear them sing, along the road with burbling springs

O young ones, untie the yellow string of the purple bag
When you dance down the road with burbling springs
Pause in delight, hear the singers, the fluttering dancing things

That come to us, imagining, what if it happens
Untying the yellow string of the purple bag we
Hear the singers, the fluttering dancing things
On the road with burbling springs

## *EMINENCE*

The grey stopped. Stood. Unmoving. Jessup leapt from the saddle.
Held the horse by the head.
Looked into her eyes. Talking softly to her. Gently unbuckling the
bridle. Taking the bit from her mouth.
Rubbing her twenty-five year old neck.

He had foaled her. From that day they had enjoyed a symbiotic
unity. I have seen her gallop across
The paddock on sighting him. Muzzling him with affection. He,
taking carrots from his pocket, he
Carried for her

The kilometre to the barn took an hour. With glazed eyes the horse
stumbled slowly along. Seemingly not
Fully conscious. At last outside her stall. She turned slightly to
Jessup. Placed her beautiful head on his
Shoulder. He enfolded her with his arms.

They stood together for a minute. Goodbyes being said. Benediction
spoken. Blessing conferred
Then very gently she fell to her knees, rolling with thoroughbred
grace to the floor. When her head hit the cobble stones she was gone

I heard the front-end loader start up shortly after and head for the
northern corner of the home paddock.

From there, as today in the sun, the twist of the river could be seen
as it reached the beach. Beyond
Light glinting on the white fringe of breaking waves

The bush telegraph had sprung into action. When the loader
returned some eight people had gathered. The scoop was pushed
close to the back of the corpse. With much effort, helped by six
men, the body was moved and secured in the scoop. The loader
backed out carefully, turning towards the newly dug grave

Tenderly the remains were laid in the grave, the soil quickly returned, until finally the grass tussocks were pushed, pressed, patted into place by the heavy knuckles of the scoop, leaving little sign of disturbance.

No words were said. Country people know when to leave space for grief. Aware, if agitated, it can rise up as a tidal wave that could drown us. We returned in silence to the house

Five days later I called and on passing the grave site saw a Wollemi pine planted on the site.

Careful husbandry of the land around. Visiting two days after I saw Jessup, rake in hand, beside the new tree. I placed my hands on his shoulders. He nodded twice. We did not speak. Words have little efficacy in the presence of such deep sorrow. A slight drizzle as the sky wept quietly with us. We stood, enfolded in heart and mind by the fragrance of this sacred place. Sacredness that Country embodies and avows

## *BEAUTY*

Then there is beauty
Compelling as the need for recognition
Elusive as the perfume of a rose
Clarity of the icicle, warmly renewing
Balm for the suffering soul

Not in its tonality alone
The nimbus of desire, gently bestowed
But in communication's depth
Of what matters, of what confers
Wonder, astonishment and meanings code

Shaping a presence of what is forever
Overwhelming, unavoidable, and fraught
However fleeting, however insubstantial
Beyond description, beyond possession
The heart of things devoutly thought

Sinking into the unconscious
Subterranean, influence continually to shine
And over years birthing essentiality
Colouring the act of breathing, of praising
This glimpsed reflection of loveliness sublime

## CENTRE

Where can the mind camp
In this wilderness into which we come
I plant my heart's hunger
Seeds of distrust and uncertainty
Growing along as I lie fallow, waiting
Aching for full grain ground into life
Bread promised across the sown
River plain, water to hand
The river gums spreading shade

When Jessup comes in the soft dusk
The fire still burning, the billy
Sending upwards signal of readiness
We will share a meal and I
Will ask my questions as to why
Hopes are crumbling, certainties fleeing
Before floods carrying disease
Wreaking havoc, leaving no place to stand secure
As if we have become dispossessed

There are rock carvings 60,000 years old, he says
They have not succumbed to wind, sun, or rain
No wilderness is eternally safe, omnipotent
It is not what is that endures
But that it is. Within its unfolding
The stamp of human feet, art etching
Which gives to the wilderness its meaning
Without which it has no understanding or
Song to sing. Be present. The centre lies here

## GREATNESS

The image rose from some unguarded vault of the unconscious
Fully displayed to startled recognition. In those days poverty was easily detected

He rode into the parking spot, working boots pushing the pedals
An ancient bicycle, rust spots glistening on mudguards in the sun

Worn workman's clothes, a fierce stare surrounded by jet black whiskers
His splayed eye looking askance at me over the slight body of his son

A small figure on the bike's crossbar, somewhat uncertain
Trusting his father totally nonetheless, in wide-eyed anticipation

Why this picture returned remains mysterious
Out of its archaic resting place in childhood

I remember the signs of evident struggle, the squinted gaze, my empathy
And most of all the fiery energies of his unspoken pride

*This is my son. I am his father. This is greatness before you*

### II

Looking down on my son below, playing with his two sons
I feel the resonance of that proud, intense communication again

Remembered, for such love is not easily found in this broken world
I saw it in a moment before me. I saw it in its naked beauty

Blazing in the eye of an afflicted worker, who carried no status
In his daily toil, triumphant in the deepest recesses of his being

Giving me words to name my own estate
*This is my son. I am his father. This is greatness before me*

And my son, living into the same love
Creating a greatness before him in his turn

Repeating a refrain that rises above poverty into wealth
*These are my sons. I am their father. This is a greatness before me*

## DOG POUND DAY

He stepped uncertainly out of the Pound's abandonment carrying a nimbus of sorrow
induced by the treachery of being no longer wanted, despite the constancy of his love and faithfulness, the sun picking up the first grey hairs along his muzzle and he, shuffling a little, a phantom limp, a stumble even, came out to meet his new family, a soft coated gentleness that, like a sign board, spoke of a willing, wanting, heart, low tailed confidence, but open again to offer what he had, all of himself,
warmth, trust, and love, longing to be included, to belong, to offer comfort

## GIVINGNESS

The essence of the one talking
Is more important to discern than
The meaning of what they say
For truth is not context or language
But an embodiment, a testimony
A sustained narrative of integrity

I was inspired by who they were
What they said soon faded away
One was filled with joy and delight
Another with committed endeavour
Here, an uncritical inclusiveness
There, a shared struggle with the poor

None of them gave much attention
To the commercial world, of making money
Pouring out their life for others, not
Conscious of doing so, in being what they
Believed they were called to be, to do
Giving to my hunger food that nourished
Without knowing they shaped my life

## FREEDOM

We were sent home early from school
The day the Second World War ended
My mother and neighbours in the street
Outside of our house, my mother crying

Remembering her brother Fred, killed
In a hospital in Tobruk when it was bombed
A child knows the difference between life and death
Is momentous, as is the destruction of tyranny

That day I learned how precious freedom is
And the price we pay for it to live among us

## STRUGGLE

It is always on the edges
Beyond the trimmed hedges

That we see clearly
Life is lived unsurely

Not mowed or raked or weeded
Precise, controlled, or seeded

A space of hazard, risk, and doubt
Within confusion, scrabbling about

Each day a test, a struggle
Without assurance of survival

From this perspective, sharp, insistent
Insight grows, wise, strong, persistent

Anticipatory resoluteness
That pays tribute to uniqueness

## *TRAVELLERS TALE*

The rays of my life, sent out in the morning
Turned at noon and began to withdraw
Back into the darkness from which they rose

The task they carried, now in sunset glow
Was not to strive but to understand
The going out, the returning again

Colours stretched out upon life's canvas
Carrying meaning's internal scheme
A structure asking to be defined

What does the canvas reveal, conceal
Its liniments stretching into counter-point
Delineating a traveller's way with steady steps

Now discerned, not foreground events
But the background architecture that
Holds the field of vision in place

The whole, a complex of belonging
Seeking to be known, deeply included
Welcomed into creation's spin

Throughout the binding thread
The traced next step, the guiding wind
Promise of a coming yet. A beginning

## LEGO

Lego pieces lie scattered across the table top
Some in technicolour clumps, others isolated, alone
Disconnected, useless, and nonplussed at the sudden change

Only minutes ago, one powerful force, a Ford Mustang
Belching black exhaust fumes onto fragile curtains
At 200 kilometres an hour

Already bright intelligence broods on the next step
Considering a fresh act of creation, omnipotent beyond imagining
Three sections constructed severally, interlocked, rocket completed

Only to see the silent plastic swept into a cotton bag
String tightened at the neck, and they, upstairs
To tooth brushes, pyjamas and darkened bedrooms

Jostled together in the cotton bag lego bits wonder if
Tomorrow they will unite again, each to its chosen place
To conquer limitless space, symbiotic with the darkened room
Planning above

## HUBRIS

Under the magic spell of early twilight
Looking back over the Wetland ponds
Streaked by descending orange and yellow shafts
Nature speaks only with a muted voice

The violence of an angry god does not thunder
Nor avenging lightning strike revengefully
No sprite moves transparently in the lifeless water
The Wattle tree, casting an antipodal shadow does not house
A healing spirit, nor does the tongued copper head
Speak to me of primal wisdom or malevolent evil
The fold of the hill slope does not shelter dragons
Numinous spirit has vanished, unlamented

The environment has been cleansed of affect
Coded now, dismissively, as land
That carriers no mystery, hides no wonderment
Sprayed, raked, and cultivated, all wildness prohibited

The symbolism of our unconscious world struggles
For oxygen, imagination dying in the fading light
The Apollinarian force of calculating reason
Our greatest and most devastating illusion
Leaving only guttered apartment blocks
Maternity hospitals and schools bombed into ruin
Driven by the furies of nationalistic hubris
The earth and its children discarded background

## IMPERMANENCE

It is the unattended moment that haunts us
The years of neglected impact mount up
Lost, slipping between our fingers unnoticed
Back into the stream of uncalled on possibility

Caught as we are in senses unweighted
Of the magic of the moment that delivered nothing
Of import in the distracted present
Saturated with possibilities wasted and unused

Why we were so distracted is hard to say
Little was defined that grew or lasted
Between then and now any bridge issueless
As a means of bringing answers

So salutary to ask, where did the years go
Memory is too unreliable to trust
Its archive, and what we gathered
Dries into nothing much upon examination

We only carry echoes, random images
Of what we sought unnamed, and what was valued
Unhelpful in the present time
Of remembering and reflection's gleaning

We do not have the means to hold surely
In life's vagaries that which is truly precious
Defensively we cherish the illusion that it matters not
Whether life was lived evasively, an unattended moment

## SHOPPING CART

She was barely higher than the shopping cart
A galaxy of rioting colour
Wrapped in innumerable layers against the cold
Pushing determinedly, stop start, stop start

Her ancient face red with effort
Grey head bowed, set to the mammoth task
Groceries stacked to the top, uncertain
Diminishing energies stretched to the limit

The cart see-sawing a wavering transition
Unfaithful to the desired line
Her burly son with guiding touches
Kept the cart aimed to her destination

He watched in love, twice her size
Giving her the gift of independence
Overseeing the granted autonomy with care
Grief already peeping from the corners of his eyes

## SOMEWHERE ELSE

It leads onto something desired, and then another detour
Down dark alleys, across fog afflicted parks
To unlighted roads, white with moonlight
And the sheer inscrutability of things

Diving into the ocean has the same effect
Of myriad pathways, defined only by passing eddies
Calling us to follow disappearing fins no more real
Than blue water sky above sea weed distortions

It is the lack of substance, ephemeral absolutes
That have no permanence, merely kindling for the fire
On cold nights of rioting stars, leading to somewhere else
Offering the promise of a permanency that will not last

## JUMPING SHOES

He was wearing his jumping shoes today
The worn Superman cloak with frayed edges
Around his shoulders

Under one arm a dinosaur
Under the other a spaceship

Singing as he came for his morning glass of milk
Stopping from time to time to give
Instructions to invisible comrades

Placing the dinosaur and the spaceship
On the table he scrambled up the kitchen stool
And quickly drank the milk, turning suddenly

Clattering down, running to the window
To watch intently, a white flock cawing
Across a sun tinged blue sky

Looking out of his window I saw only
Burning eucalyptus bush, brown treacherous floods
Overlain by a grey mantle of pollution

Praying that in any future he must conquer
He would always have a song to sing and
Trusted companions on the way

Who share his dreams, both old and new
And are, like him, wearing their jumping shoes

## *ENTITLEMENT*

How is it possible to penetrate that sense of entitlement
Which is impervious to negotiation, convinced of superiority
Dismissive of those who lack will, or skill, or power
Convinced they deserve what they desire. A meritocracy

Entitlement only has cogency when it is universal
A golden seam within compassion's grounded-ness
Not by claim of celebrity, achievement, or even status
Given deep within the sovereign fold of humanness

Nobility resides in the poor, the disabled, the hopeless
To be honoured, cherished, protected as fragile seed
Entitlement is their birthright, their inheritance
Not by virtue or uniqueness but by need

In the simple act of kindness, affirmation of the other
As one with us, our bone and flesh and kin
A mutuality which births communal enlightenment
Honouring by inclusiveness a true entitlement within

## BREAKNECK SPEED

We come into the world at breakneck speed
Anxious to get on with it, only to find
That time is a snail. There is a system in place
Regulated by Grandfather clocks of measured
Ticks and equally measured tocks

The hours creep by, the days inch along
Weeks in step with glaciers
Months limping with damaged fetlocks
Into the slow foxtrot of the years

We look ahead to serried ranks of decades
Trying to push the weight of time
Filled with adolescent urgencies that
Do not want to miss multiplying agendas
Fraught with destiny and waves of surfing brine

But now time's enigma rears up, adjusts
The time frame is a wind beyond believing
We occupy with slugs and snails a temperate zone
Watching the days pass at breakneck speed
The steed of time galloping as if in pursuit

When the change occurred I was not watching
Content to ease into the distance run
Failing to grasp time now outstripped me
Wrapping up the days, whipping the lazy months, scattering
The years, and hours so fast little can be done

Small tasks confining time to shopping trolleys
And time, for its part, a race in nano seconds
Leaving us behind, making up for those days
When slow steps lead to open possibilities
We could not reach in time. Now dashing past

## SOMETIMES

Sometimes it happens
In the minute of reflection
A single thread glows in the dark

The beginning and end obscure
In a complexity of speculation
Bearing a knot of certainty

Nothing that truly matters
Is lost in the weaving
Of a searching life

Nor does the road end
To which the signs
Without names and distances point

Only the warm luminosity
Of assurance prevails
While all else fades away

## MILKING SHED

In the miking shed Jessup became philosophical
As creamy milk foamed into steel containers
The cow cannot live in the past or future
Only in this present moment. Satisfaction for all its striving
Tomorrow it begins again, without awareness of then and later
A repetitive cycle leading to this daily climax twice

We also cannot live in the past or future
Existence is a tenancy in the present
Striving for worthy ends, deep satisfaction
But we have the capacity to enter into
The very nature of being, and to choose
Our way reflectively into a different tomorrow

We do not escape toil or repetition
Limits are set. Birth, suffering, ageing, death
But there are horizons, knowledge, awareness
That reach beyond the facticity of the now
A resonance of beyond. He smiled
We can separate the cream from the milk

## KALEIDOSCOPE

It was too quick for us
As we mastered one stage
The environment, without, within
Changed dramatically

We began again, fretfully, with new tasks
Unexpected challenges, unforeseen crises
A learning curve seeking security to trust
Only to find requirements change again

From one peak attained
We saw, surprisingly, another range
More distant, higher, intimidating
Needing new skills, fresh enterprise

As if walking on ice cracking
At each step, more threatening
At each crossing, the bank unattainable
The sense of struggle to keep balanced

Now the final change, showing clearly
We are once again on the plain
As confronted always by possibility
Filled with cherished memories of the climb


## LOTUS

The problem, a pattern of action and impasse
Offering only a cold, objective world
Intimidating as indifferent chance
By which gathering stones, generations have toiled
To little or no discernible advance
Shackled by illusions doomed to be foiled

What then of the intricacies of the Lotus
The Buddha rising out of importunity
To speak of enlightenment and mindfulness
According to the rhythm of one's innate ability
Not fate or destiny or happenstance
But shaping individuation, fruit of diversity

Weaving a self of singular enduring
From chores and secretly inspired events
Having more to do with synchronicity
Than algorithms of constrained intent
Following a measured beat, spelling correct
Of physical laws, birthing cause and effect

What then of the beauty of the Mandala
The taste of water, tasteless, giving life
Tumbling of the rock fall, the scattering of mice
Upon the wanton air beguiling fragrances of spice
To bring into a focus of delight
Inwardness and outwardness balanced aright

## BLACKBERRY HARVEST

The green bushes of tangled blackberry
Cover the gentle slope along the
River backwater, under tall gum protection
It being harvest season, armed to the teeth
Prepared to repel all comers

We, ready, with long sleeves, wide brimmed
Hats, protective glasses, approach cautiously
Suddenly battle is engaged, without trumpets
Equipped with buckets we enter in, sunlight
Glinting on purple-blue fruit deep beneath

Within the thick green foliage hidden ambush
Thorns penetrate protective clothing
Scratches across arms, legs, and faces
Deep penetration into vulnerable flesh
As teetering dangerously, we fill our buckets

Out of their hiding places squadrons of bush flies
Assaulting eyes, ears, mouth, and nose
From the river behind kamikaze mosquito hordes
Arise, moving to attack, seemingly impervious to
Spray defence and verbal abuse

Retreating at last, mission accomplished
We visit hospital stations for betadine protection
Band aids, and field bandages applied
Walking slowly across bare paddocks to the
Farm house, heat waves following us home

At noon, under sun cheating canvas spread
We gather in shade, consuming the usual
Bread and cheese, washed down with ginger beer
To the victors the spoils. Plump, juicy blackberries
Covered with fresh cream. The customary toast

We rise, spoons filled to the brim
With dark treasure won
*Here's to skin in the game,* said Jessup
Delight across his features, breeze rustling his hair
Scratches, bites, and pain forgotten

## IN AND OUT

We are not constant
Slipping in and out of time
With notions of eternity
The endless void, the silent Other
Who speaks within the timeless now

In and out of shifting perception
Time passing, undetected, unexplored
With myriad small miracles bidding
For our attention, curative and healing
Awakening our distraction into care

In and out of reason
Escaping by imagination
The cruel tyranny of logic's snare
Freeing into the air exotic hopes
Inside and outside of time

In and out of materiality
Nightly call-up to the flashing screen
Tranquillised by media fantasticals
Obsessive focus on desire and dreams
Not understanding what is never said

Only to recognise on the way to bed
The emptiness of an existence made absurd
Perceiving what transcends its banal dance
By virtue of the night's integrity
The slow drift of Minerva's owl in moon light

## REFLECTION ON ECCLESIASTES 3

Is it true that everything
Is suitable for its time
When that which is
Already has been
That which is to be
Already is

So in time, the time we inhabit
We live timelessly
Repeating patterns as if new
Hoping for those things
We already have
Trying to find all things
Suitable, amidst everything
That has its allotted time
And seems eternally elusive

In this timeliness
Of suitability
God passes, seeking
What has gone by
To that still point
Which is to be and
Already is

Past and future
In our minds
Nothing to be added
Nothing to be taken away
Everything underlining
It is suitable
For its time

The dying that we
Might live
The gathering of stones

In a time of throwing away
Here is the riddle of suitability
Suitable for what
To time's servitude

Or is it possible
A gift not understood
Time is given to us
That which we call now
For everything this is its season

www.ingramcontent.com/pod-product-compliance
Lightning Source LLC
Chambersburg PA
CBHW012006090526
44590CB00026B/3894